ERASED BY SHEEP

ERASED BY SHEEP

ANDREW FOSTER

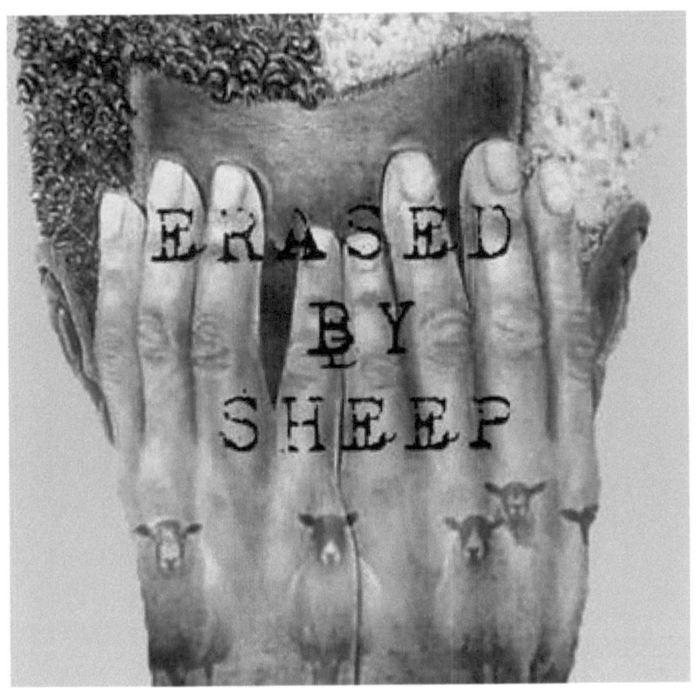

Beauty and the Beast Publishing

for
everyone who exists

Table of Contents

Foreword

I'm a recovering English teacher. I also love to write, and I find poetry the most challenging, engaging, and spiritual landscape for the written word. I can teach grammar, diagram a sentence, proofread a manuscript, all those necessary and plodding things.

Poetry engages my wings.

I am blessed to have had a couple of gentle and brilliant professors who challenged me to accept the responsibility that poetry places on us to deeply experience and to wonder and wander through meaning. One of my favorite singers, Billie Holliday, said, "I never sing a song the same way twice." Her courage is the courage of poetry: Permission for discovery. Permission for exploration without destination. The song is the thing, and each singing leads into a slightly different harbor for the heart.

Andrew Foster is a friend. We've spoken many times, and we both dropped our shields early on, so we have nothing to protect. My understanding and sense of connection with Andrew comes with the sound of his words on the page as much as with the sound of his voice and the video of his face. He has taken the plunge to drop any filters that might impede what he needs to blossom in his writing.

Andrew's work is a path and a tumble in the same walk—often the same run—as he understands cadence and that poetry is meant to be heard, to be mouthed, sung, really, so the words carry physicality as well as meaning. Please, read his work aloud to be true to his possibilities.

Writing takes courage. Writing poetry takes great courage. A leap of words always is predicated on a leap of faith: I hold nothing in my hands, but let it all go, let it all grow, and I trust that I do not need to control the ripples, only create them. Andrew is fierce in his willingness to get out of the way of his truth.

I still pick up *Poetic Declarations*, his previous book. I keep it close to my desk. I can reach it with hardly a lean, so I can take a sip or a healthy belt of his words and be reminded and re-explored.

Thank you, Andrew, for asking me to introduce *Erased by Sheep*. Wow.

Mac Bogert

Introduction

I'm told to lead by example,
in a place where high grass is parted
in a new direction.

As I stare out my caged window,
I see gated trails leading to perdition,
yet I'm asked to lead in a new direction.

How can I get people to look inside
themselves while inside to find ways outside
the perimeters of their potential?

How can I lead when their minds are intertwined
with yours? You lead with criminal intent and subjectivity
and appear as a pillar of society.

If anyone is offended who fits the description,
I care less without regret of your conquest to
divide willing minds who seek to unify for the greater good.

For family.
For nature.
For humanity.

I apologize for my gray silence
against perceptions that delineates imagination to
shape creative spaces where liberation is needed.

I apologize for trusting colorless creeds.

When we war, we imprison innocent people
in the name of sanctions and land
but call it freedom.

Anyone who defines a
race of people as the
source of sickness, we imprison.

Then you tell growing minds to stop listening,
stop listening to lies and dreams.
Visions only see things that it imagination.

Pillars shape narratives.

We are tools of our pillars,
not because of our erasure,
but because of corrupt pathos.

They create their own poetry
alluding to narratives without questioning,
leaving open assumptions for preceding stanzas.

My incarcerated people have inherited your ways.

We are divided within by the
ties that bind our thoughts into
thinking we're better than the next.

So we oppress our neighbor and ourselves.

How can we move forward when law and order
police our thoughts, individuality, goals,
and mishaps?

But you ask me to lead people in a new direction.

Alarms

Things that strike fear. Things that accelerate. Warning signs without warning. Deform postures of fear or apparent frame of mind affecting one's thoughts.

Living in Clefts

In shade we wait our turn to hunt.
Every season is Red November made
for thanksgiving as we praise dusk
with contemporary art that paints
trees to the image of deported branches.

Branches keep us safe from the shepherd's staff.
From below, we hear their footsteps treading the
dry leaves, making paths to pave trails
we once lived until somatic difference
cause division among creatures.

We dine outside of grasslands where
grass is gritted sand, spiked flowery
buds rough on our tongues knitted
from pine needles that once were
grazed above for the open sun.

How can the wilderness be ungrateful
when freshness of curled docks
outer layer caresses field pennycresses,
and dandelions grow subtly?

The burdocks account for our world's
arousal, halos circle around teeth
muzzling the primal fury
of our mouths; unholy and profane
to the bowels releasing tasteful waste.

We're ill leopards whose spots are chimer
blends of parody myths for soiled stains.

Millennial Rain

Standing on a peak.
Watching trees bloom green clouds from
the violence of rain.

Write Right

A teacher once told me to hold my pencil right.
I told her maybe the pencil is hold my hand wrong.
She then said, you write like you're left-handed with
your right hand. I didn't know right determines left other than
direction. Then I said, when pencils are
sharpened, lead sprouts without water.

The Wolf in the Wall

I

It stares at me with impale eyes
with blood on its fangs, hoping
to see if I break lace and
hang my sanity in threads.

It watches as if a flock of
geese by the pond waiting
for bread, yet its mouth
salivates for raw meat.

Still the wolf wonders if I'm part
of the pack, even though I built
my lair in walls like a
snake's burrow. But you continue

to stare at my shallow eyes that
bring color to your pupils, hypnotize
from a serpent's trance, embalm
when we lay eggs to destroy cages.

Our Past Becomes Us

Yesterday, I had a dream I was reliving the 90s. At the end of my dream, there was a picture of me and my nephews. The past will always be a part of who we are no matter what. But should we let the past control our future? Should we erase it? Should we reshape? Only the traveler should ask.

Before Now

An evil eye always glances flashes.
All my friends were people walking
virtuously in lines hand to hand, should to
shoulder, carrying our warmth to rivers
where no one advised us of beds to lay.
Narrow smiles grant passage from looks
giving as a rehearsed script signed by
said director who cuts rashes out of throats.

Dancing with Shadows

When I was walking through the museum, I noticed the color art. There was no muse to push my thoughts to know or comprehend the different colors. In my eyes, I see creative calligraphy, a pleasing coax vision, square and rectangular windows explaining seasons of compromised eyes.

Then I looked down at the pearl marble floors, a faint whistle as if the ocean's hum to moons. I closed my eyes hoping for waves. I lay in the colorful limestone, becoming part of art as the whistle went from faint to rustle. I lift my head up and opened my eyes: The art became me.

The colors moved when I moved. Every shade of red gleamed as if it knew my frustrations. Every blue, green, and gray penetrated the red's gleam as if culturing a turquoise gem. When I walked away, it followed. When I raised my hand, it raised its hand. We both sat down, looking at each other: both worthy of imitation.

Rust Heaven

The sky is deadly,
with no welcoming entrance
from the hell we praise.

Sheltered

In the land of sheep, we lurk in meadows
of white shade, blemished oaks

with sappy grey vines that overcome Eden
while snatching up roots from dirtless guilt.

Something weightless and inexperienced
when connected to beauty that

entices us to hunger for garments
laid was wool carpet embraced with glory.

We're erased by narratives,
open fields capture the sheep's brilliance,

but our story remains in caves
where we plot and watch blemishes unfold.

What Does Chaos Look Like?

It looks like a bunch of lines intersecting in every direction with no
ending. Different colors exploding simultaneously. People running in
every direction. Planes crashing, screams, Earth spinning off its axis.

Wisdom from the Deprave

In the church of Pentecost,
I learned without searching
the letters that preaches tent
builders and carpenters are chosen people.
"Yes Lord!" said the preacher
with Pompeii Olive Oil absorbed in his face
as if the shining of a spirit granted him power.
I remember sitting for hours waiting for the great
tribulation. Instead, the preacher's words called
me up in clouds where rain rests.
I understood this rapture as a bored rhythm
without substance: words of emotions structured
for eager ears to hear.

Then I aged in mind and physique,
critiquing what the preacher preaches,
gaining knowledge from slaves whereas I
was taught to obey my master's house.
"Yes, you're a slave unto the Lord!" said the preacher
as the offering plate is passed from hands that
bore chains from birth.

I learn from slaves: Sallie Holley, an apostle,
a woman, an abolitionist, a lecturer.
I learn from slaves: A. Phillip Randolph,
who passed his labor to M.L.K.
I learn from slaves: Malcolm Little
branded with X by all means.
I learn from slaves: Gloria Jean Watkins,
may she rest in bells and hooks.
I learn from slaves: Nadine Godimier,
writer and revered in South Africa,
who taught us to go beyond Eden.
I learn from slaves: Audre Lorde,
James Baldwin, Angel Davis.
Dismantlers of flawed structures,
building frames of love,
standing firmly on the right to exist.

Declaration; who once marked beasts with swords,
sacrifice for others to see freedom as a
creative path to peace: I stand courageously
against preachers who fear the enslaved.

Pillar Ruins

The body is self-demolition,
instruments waiting to fade,
grandfather's timepiece and rushed matter.

Believe when on says we're easily led.
Believe when arms act as anchors
draped to depths of sinking sand.

The worst effort is losing intuition,
knowing a master medium massages
spines to ease dancing minds.

Years of heel-to-toe formal balls,
man-on-man hands inspect nakedness
shaping Adams without Eves.

Lungs feed soil while
plants sing labor
until will is broken.

Broken Jazz

When a woman is at the end of her rope,
she uses dust to pierce ears
improvised by dissonant pitch.

If the note is off-key, she then
hums hymns on weak lines
conducting sounds of broken measures.

It runs deep in her soul,
seeps in her bones, causing
her rib to sing sorrow songs.

She laments skirts and hallow heels,
cracking floors in sections,
while men sing prolonged melodies.

If she has a choice,
she'll settles for silence,
instead of broken measures.

Then she realizes men
spare their ribs to change
women's pitch.

Token Lady

Out of spite spitting words
our ears consume iron.
All is salt from water
not tears that irritate
eyes to shut a wink.
At times I blink repeats
of her-story as a sheet
wrapped around her open
wound, closing off all life.
Inside she's a fortress,
expelling her after-birth due
to selfishness. She erupts
truffle words to assure her
generous tales of supremacy
that white-washed our hearts
to believe we're others, separate
from droplets of blood-kin. Though
a spokesperson, she continues to hide
in polished ponds as tokens rust
and sink.

Colors

I once read Bluing the Linens by Laurie Ann Guerrero and realized colors derive from somewhere other than what's told to us. In certain circumstances and conditions, plants if not nurtured properly decay and turn brown, when once upon a time it was only a seed. The point is, nothing starts off pure nor does a certain color assign itself to what's considered pure.

When Walls Talk

II

The last time I slept in walls
I fasted from loud calls of the
guard's lockdown.

The guard's key indicates a jingle,
counting steps toward heads
attached to rooms for his safety.

If the head loosens, he'll run fro
cover, leaving the head to roam in
puddles of boot polish.

It happens when police flee
from war cries. Black face comes
in many forms when painted,

except your uniform is breast-plated
with armor from saber
whips and black people who

boot-lick to capture a face
descended from ash: your fire
only burns when massa comes.

Ash will always be underfoot.

Untitled

Three of the most essential tools
that should be in every lawyer's
toolbox is silence, active listening,
and critical thinking.
—James H. Fierberg

Muted by words overbear the listener, so I sacrifice
my words as a head cut off and burned to demons
in hope to possess a skillful spell.

Sordid jinx, throbbing tapping gavels, scratches air
to a point where order isn't part of
physics, nor does matter eyewitness to testimony,
especially earshot's to one's eardrums.

To contest, I resign from parse mistakes.

Legal language put together only wrinkles the
brain, putting to rest thoughts that may
bring premise of what may seem valid.

Guilt

When crime is present,
be a witness to its guilt,
till it turns on you.

Hero

The governor said he will not allow convicts to taunt law enforcement's families as if they are the only victims. Not really. He didn't say that...But he made sure to fence policies awry to time spent in cell nooses.

Does the public know where heroes lie? They lay their courage on backs without heads, arms without hands, waists without legs, bodiless torsos who can't see their harm is promoted by the tongues of villains. Pop always said never trust a tainted tongue drenched with lemons. I say: heroes play on the weak to justify their efforts as heroic. I'm stressed. I'm stressed. What's taking place is an orator's mission to skin backs with scrapers, leaving spinal cords to dangle for forage. The public thinks not. Because of lazy thinking, the minds of many struggle to find skulls when though is freely given.

Georgia Out My Mind

Why Georgia? Native names of streets and highways? Deceased red clay? God's belt that needs fastening? Food that gives soul? Georgia doesn't have soul.

Married to Nothing

I held your hand only to
remind myself that age is ancient
glass, broken spectacles of
blurred sight.

My love for you was engraved
from the essence of sage where
every line and crevice gives
off scented travels.

I pray for the day we meet
again to vent about times we
missed due to neglectful rambles
of other people's expense.

I can't change passed shortcomings
that cause green flame to kindle
mixed feelings to over-burdened
sadness.

I apologize for keeping heat
within myself only to share
it with cold reefs above
water. Now you're gone.

Time Moves in Windows

Windows show us our destination.

Me and Mr. Jackson always stare out the window,
mapping out our daily travels of the world.

Where to Mr. Jackson?
How about a tour of Vermont?

Never been, but I heard about the
mulberry trees that march to Maine.

We can build a small rustic cabin,
it has to have a rustic feel.

I agree.

Didn't you say you liked those A-frame houses?

Yeah, the design reminds me of small
wooden pyramids in the forest.

I see.

So what about tomorrow, Mr. Jackson,
where are we going?

Don't know. But life is moving
while we're stuck in the middle.

The gray hairs on elders
is a poetic investment to life.

All their words are connected
to past experience: a spoken word

for our time to build theatres
of worlds as an act of guild.

In life, we hope to be a part
of its circle not because we're

forced from pressures to live in
tunnels, but to bring vision,

uplifting those left in the center,
bringing them to stages where life

gives chance with open arms
and not spectated endings.

Numb to Slaughter

A crash is the sound violence
to invisibility—not peripheral vows
near hell-bound woes.

True it may feel like
ulcers to ears playing drums
off-beat to diminish.

As long as open sores
welcome mountains, its pace
sets shins below rocky caps.

Author Bio

ANDREW FOSTER is a poet and scholar. His poems and essays have appeared in *Bizcatalyst 360, Humanity @ Work Foundation, The Angel Experience, and Otel Universe.* He is also the author of *Poetic Declarations, 2020 Sublimes*, and *Sable Haven*.